URBAN BALLADS

THE COLLECTION

BY

ALEXANDER ROBERTSON

‘A shared delight in the spoken word.’

Grosvenor House
Publishing Limited

This book is published by
Grosvenor House Publishing Ltd
Link House
140 The Broadway, Tolworth, Surrey, KT6 7HT.
www.grosvenorhousepublishing.co.uk

A CIP record for this book
is available from the British Library

ISBN 978-1-80381-228-1

For Freda, my forever first-time reader.

URBAN BALLADS

A sparkling mixture of narrative poems gathered around the faults, fragilities and triumphs of the individual as social being.

Populated by character and situation, they are theatre in condensed form, providing the reader with the opportunity beyond quiet contemplation, to tell their story out loud, alone or in a crowd.

By language which promotes itself as being clever, beautiful, insightful and communicable, these lines seek to master that rarest of achievements, which is to be popular and profound.

Contents

MISTER UNIVERSE

The return trip was his last trip,
And possibly the riskiest of all.
Having survived world dangers with the help of strangers,
He was now going back,
To confront the hostility of friends.

He had been warned by an old time tripster,
No matter where in the world you might roam.
Never to expect, the stories you collect,
Will be of interest to anyone back home.

But he was going home as a listener.
A 'ready to fit in and hear all'.
A 'tell me again about the night of the streetlights black out',
And 'what was that about the neighbour's wall?'.

He was given a great welcome; bought pints as one of their own.
The talk congenial and never ending,
The nights loud and long.
He had revived them, the locals, bright and eager to join in,
Not for the tales he was telling them,
But the stories they were telling him.
As the only one who hadn't heard them,
In the last thirty years.

After a month of it, he was up to date.
Then the talk became nothing much, and much the same the next day.
Leaving the space in conversation, for what he might have to say,
If they hadn't preferred the silence, to him telling them,
Where he had been while away.

He knew it, he expected it,
He had been warned, but not on the effect of it.
Which diminished him, reduced him,
To being the lesser for having gone away.
His recent years, the missing years,
Because they were not theirs.

But he knew he was better than that.
He was an import of everywhere he had been.
Coming in with the swell of the Indian Ocean,
Reflecting the heat of an African sun.

It was already there in the conversation,
A Tamarind seed on the Great Divide.
When they said 'boozer' he said 'bar'.
When they went 'doon the chippy',
He spoke 'platters of 'fruits de mer'.

It was unsettling for the locals,
To have one of their own, they no longer knew,
Come as a stranger, and talk of elsewhere,
Placing the world between them and what was before...
That, which, it was time to restore.

So they did what they always did with strangers.
They made him a character and gave him a name.
'Mister Universe' they called him,
Which he never got to hear,
Because they united around the joke,
Only when he wasn't there.
They had made him an island, safe to visit but not to stay.
Someone to be quiet in his company, until he was wished away.

Which he eventually was by his own deciding.
He had no place in a town which spurned,
His choice to come home, and remain where he'd been.
In going, he knew he would never return.

Except on the night of his leaving, they were united at last.
Best pals forever as they waved him off,
Promising to write, and hoping he might,
Be back soon to the welcome he left.

He found by going why he had returned,
Which he took with him as he went.
That fond farewell stuck with him as a marker,
That would grow by the distance he kept.
And as the memory grew weaker, of how he had been treated,
Given time, he might just possibly want to come back.

PERISHABLE FRUIT

It was the simplest exchange in a cafe,
No more than 'What'll you have dear?'
And 'a coffee for me, please'
He a customer, and she serving,
What more could it possibly be?

Except for the whirring inside his head,
Spinning from nothing at all.
Beyond her pleasing familiarity,
Awakening in him the possibility,
Forming a gossamer thread around them,
Unbroken as she walked away.

He'd led himself to believe that she liked him,
Without evidence supporting the claim.
Except. when asked what he was having,
He was encouraged to believe,
Her interest in him responding
Was contact, given and received.
And when seeing her return with his coffee,
Took that as proof of what he wanted to believe.

And there it began where it ended. The bill paid as he left,
No regret at her leaving, he knew she was with him yet.
In his mind along with his shopping, wrapped up as perishable fruit,
To be opened at his own choosing
And make of it what he would.
The scene as remembered,
He a customer and she serving
Best before closing.

MILD PROTEST

Subjecting myself to some scrutiny,
Of the comfortable life I lead.
I have allowed myself the notion,
Of doing something for those in need.

I hit on the option of street protest,
Which identifies the blame as elsewhere.
And with nothing to do on a Saturday,
Could be experience, my just being there.

I had always admired the colour,
the pageantry of the marching band.
Leading the banner waving purpose,
Of a people walking hand in hand.

Why wasn't I among them, I asked,
That recruiting army of volunteers?
Marching along while I stayed home,
Was it me they were marching for?

I looked for a passion, a particular cause,
That could lift me from the sofa,
To join that glorious peoples protest song,
And have me shouting in chorus?

I thought I'd be driven by anger,
The injustice, the blatant abuse.
But I found nothing much to upset me,
And, I know that's hardly an excuse, but...

I had to examine their causes
Some of which I couldn't agree.
Some I would gladly have thrown stones at,
But I still thought, there must be a campaign for me.

I employed a mental balance,
Weighed the just cause, societies gain,
Against the inconvenience for me personally,
Walking in the wind and the rain.

I'm afraid to say, I came out in favour of comfort,
And my argument supported the same,
Having looked at their causes, I found mostly losses,
And something wrong with all of their claims.

From the feckless poor to corrupting dictators,
The blatant thieving of the food bank waiters.
All on the make, and out to take...,
I'm sorry, but that did it for me.

But I'm still active in their campaigns,
Now I've taken my support indoors.
I'm there every night in front of the telly,
Screaming at stuff, you wouldn't believe,

And without need of transport to get there,
And the fumes kept behind the screen.
I see myself as saving the planet,
And now identifying as Green.

That settles me back on the sofa,
Knowing I couldn't do more.
Than lie through most of it,
As much as I did before.

LOVE'S INVENTION

When I come close to forgetting,
What love is, and how it's come to be named.
I look to my music listing
For the means of memory regained.

I find trite words, simple melody,
In a song three minutes long,
Allow some singer, the power
To lift me,
Up to falling in love again

I get there by streaming,
In sentiments closest to me,
The shrill tender cry of remembered love,
The fleeting glance of new romance.
A minute of that, and I'm launched, set free,
Pushed helpless, drifting
Drowning in a deep, nostalgic sea.

I take a whisky for the trip,
A glass, maybe two.
Because I want to be reckless in falling
Indifferent to where I'll be

When it wantonly seduces me,
Bright flash images, and teeth to the heart.
Stupid in love, and blindingly,
Back to my own faltering start.
When I knew that spike of nature,
Know it now, just the same.
Proof I'm still taken by love,
Still punctured by its pain...

Never grown older by the sense of it
What else can draw my tears,
But the bitter regret,
From having left,
Those lost love longing years.

Because that was the height of it,
Pitch fever, never, since attained.
A force forged in bewilderment,
Of passion burned, or simply put,
Youth with its head turned.

I go back to capture the essence,
To hold and contain, what was mine.
To seal that stream, and prevent escape
Of the spirit which fades with the whisky's effect
But I can never extend the length of it
Beyond the singer's allotted time

I'm left to praise the song,
Which offered the ready guide.
A tap of the screen,
Flashback to what's been,
A taste that never remains,
And can't be again.

But I know where to find it,
Vicarious delusional might be.
But as real as the breath within me,
And constant as memory

But it leaves me wondering why I didn't stay,
In that blissful remembered state,
If the best was in the beginning
Why not the beginning again, and again?
Or is the pain of falling out, to fall in,
Worse than the gain?

If that beauty which first attracts,
Is a trick to get you in,
And infatuation your best friend, doesn't stay to the end,
Of the party which started that incomparable love,
But leaves you to make your own way.
What's left for the romantic, and foolish,
Who are always on call?
Do they define love wherever they find love,
Or are they failing whenever they fall?

I'll never know because my recurring affairs
Are just a tableaux played out to music.
But one girl I met, is with me yet,
Proving something more enduring.

If love first, is simple,
And marriage later, complex,
What does it take to qualify,
(Ours was a double first)
In matters modern and arcane,
To find that, sometimes love,
Goes by another name.

LAUGHING AT A FUNERAL

I saw a funny thing at a funeral once,
And it made me want to laugh
But I didn't, because I knew I shouldn't,
Out of respect for the past life,
Of someone I knew when alive.

It wasn't easy, keeping the mirth within,
With the muscles in the face forming a grin.
Which I suppressed by miming a frown,
Fixed till the first hymn was announced,
When I allowed my laughter to drown,
By singing out loud.

What is it that makes us want to laugh when we shouldn't?
Is it funnier when not allowed?
Or is laughter like a sneeze
That won't be denied.
And if it is,
Compresses inside,
Liable to burst out,
When least qualified?

It was the coffin carried from the hearse
To those of us waiting inside
By six men, relations I think,
That had me laughing,
If it had been allowed.

One of the bearers, was shorter than the others,
By a clear distance, shoulder to coffin.
To close the space above him,
And make contact with his burden,
He had his arm bent, and palm upward,
Like a waiter, carrying a tray.

As they turned towards the dias, I saw his subterfuge,
The awkwardness of his shoulder lifting walk.
And although within the group, he kept the funeral look,
I knew him, for what he was.

Where does the inappropriate laugh come from?
Is it a truth greater than ourselves?
Should we allow, whatever comes out,
And be about us what that tells?

No, that wouldn't be me.
I am what I want others to see.
Why I held face disciplined, character defined,
As a mourner, respectful of the occasion,
And of the acquaintance who died.

But years looking back, I still have a giggle,
Yes, even laugh out loud, at that image still clear,
Of the short arsed pall bearer and what he wanted to hide,
But I can never remember the coffin, or who was inside.

Proving laughter lasts longest,
Especially when not allowed.

ANGER MANAGEMENT

Looking for improvement, I sought to be,
A person different from the one ascribed to me,
By friends, who, lately, had me accused,
Of being a ‘grumpy old bastard’,
(a term often misused).

Although I couldn’t deny,
On occasion words have let fly,
But bad tempered and loud,
Is not coming from me.
But a label attached on delivery,
A malicious adhesion, which,
Can’t be excised by surgery.

Been with me since my youth,
A condition distorting truth.
Beginning small, sometimes called,
‘Impatience’, I lived with it,
Did me no wrong.
In fact I used it, stopped me,
Standing in queues too long.

But with age it has developed,
Mutated itself by division.
From the simple to the sinister, born,
Twins, sometime known,
As 'Irritation' and 'Temper',
Insult added to offensive,

Parasites which can be lazy and inert,
A useless appendage seemingly in remission,
But turn uncontrollable, if revived,
By the slightest provocation.

For years I've lived with the complaint
Taken the blame for its behaviour.
Witnessed distress, cleaned up the mess,
Of another embarrassing outburst.
From the two inside, fighting to be heard.

It's an ailment without sympathy,
I'm never believed when I say it's not me.
I express regret but don't expect,
Any understanding of the effect,
Bile has on the workings,
Of the person I want to be.

A word misplaced can set them off,
Some thoughtless action, others easily ignore.
But not by 'Irritation', quick to take offence,
Setting off ' 'Temper', which, aroused and,
Supposedly in my defence,
Betrays my meaning, and uses my voice,
To damn me as inappropriate and loud.

A flash of madness, and it's over, soon as begun.
I'm left to promise it won't happen again.
But where are they to express regret,
The two who played the major part,
With me, ejected from pub and screen?
They're asleep of course, their work is done,
Back to being denied, as if they had never been.

This is a deadly chain, if unrestrained,
Can lead to anger, violence and death.
I don't want to exaggerate the strength of it.
I've never had it that bad.
But I worry for my future
If I'll have any friends left.

So on advice from them that remain,
I'm taking the passive course,
Which I hope to tell you about,
In another verse.

ON PLATFORM

On giving a first talk in front of her peers,
And the professors, the lecturers, those,
Who had taught her the subject, she was aware,
That in hearing her, it might appear,
She knew more than they

But her enthusiasm for speaking,
Was driven by her own discovery,
Of a concept creative and new
Of which, she hoped nobody else had thought,
Certainly, she had never seen it reviewed.

She typed out in large font, the text,
In case her memory failed
Which was highly unlikely because as academic writing,
She wasn’t speaking from what was written,
But echoing her imaginative soul.

To be doubly sure of her pitch,
She read to herself what had to be said,
And there experienced a first measure of doubt,
Not on the sustainability of her thesis, but on its description,
How it would come over, when spoken out loud.

Which gave rise to questions,
She put to the same text.
What is not there which should be?
What is there that should not...?
She had a suspicion but to be certain,
She went back to other's writing.
Leaders in her field who were successful and read.
Meaning they had been published
As acknowledged experts.

With some relief she saw the difference,
Not difficult to fix and correct.
Hers was too short and succinct,
There's longer and more complex.

The change she made was not plagiarism but the simple insert,
Of the bigger five syllables and more.
Words that stood out by their length alone,
Had muscle and demanded to be heard.
And with this added bulk to her thesis,
Standing testament to diligence of research
Her confidence was quickly restored.

In front of the assembled audience,
She started sprightly enough
The introduction was her own, and setting the tone
By her revelations in a specialisation,
Her discourse was on course to the end.

Till she met the first of the inserts, and slowed,
To clamber over what couldn't be got round,
Tackling words as strangers, highlighting the dangers,
Of ignorance professing profound.

She had entered the circumlocution of erudition,
A dark forest of faux friends mispronounced.
Over conjugation she stumbled, by synthesis humbled
Till crawling to a confutation ending text,
She was met with the applause she didn't expect...

And the applause continued to the bar
Where drinks were bought, by those she sought,
To impress and thought she hadn't.
And even with the second glass in her hand, she didn't understand,

The congratulations and talk of publication,
But when her promotion was mooted,
And as much as decided,
She fell in with the consensus, opportunity provided…

But she had stumbled on the secret
Of how to impress, and why,
By using the words, of her superiors, themselves,
Who, hearing where they had once been denied,
Now spoken by someone so young,
Were delighted to see it revived.

But the weight of those words, combined,
Smothered the original spark
That had prompted her speaking before she took to reading
What it was like to be everybody else.

But the creative echo goes on forever,
And will come again,
But fainter on return
And more easily denied.

TALKING TO MYSELF

Recently I was taken back 30, 40, 50, years, to that young apprentice standing there,
Myself as I was then, and me back there as an older man.
Affording him the opportunity I never had,
Of mentor, guide, example to him for the years ahead.

I knew him as myself from early photographs,
But he didn't know me, as I was for him yet to be.
But I hoped by my values, he would come to believe,
The truth of my worth, in him, as the best he will achieve.

I wasn't there to criticise or dismiss,
The wild ambitions I knew he had,
But to trim the more outrageous of the schemes,
And guide his extravagant aims back within his means.

I wanted to spare him the hurt of the wasted years,
Chasing that which he would never outrun,
To pause and acknowledge where he was lacking,
And be the better within a lesser team.

I was there as an example of security and content,
Happiness measured by degree and increment.
He wanted fame; I was that within my own home,
Loved for my losses, not my gains.

Of course he didn't listen to me,
I never expected he would.
I was to him, small beer, bitter
For what I hadn't, but knew I should.

I could have told him then 'Don't mock!'
'I am what you will be!' But I held back for fear,
Of killing what he genuinely conceived,
As fate, fuelled by a fantasy that anything can be.
What I offered for life, couldn't begin to meet what he believed.

I was the disappointment he hadn't yet met,
So I slipped away, back to a later date,
Where I would meet myself, closer to my own age,
And share agreement on the choices made.

Leaving the generation divide abundantly clear,
Why the young don't listen, and the old don't hear.

WORDS BETWEEN THEM

Two strangers meeting in a bar,
Fell into a conversation
Which hadn't gone far
Before being stopped on request, by one,
Pressing to answer please by explaining,
What it was the other was actually saying.

Coming from different parts of this island,
They spoke the same language with a different code
Entry, which as a means of communication by
Pronunciation and enunciation, bewildered the listener
Not familiar with the formula observed.

Reluctant to moderate how they had been taught
In their manner of speaking, believing it correct
They pursued the same idiom by repeating and louder,
Till what they said, couldn't be heard,
By talking at the same time, and over each other

In order to promote the way he spoke,
It was thought clever by the visitor to adopt
The furrowed brow and puzzled look
At the other's attempt to be understood.
Pleading sorry, what was that, and shaking the head
As one who knows better than what's being said.

That made the local determined, to enunciate every word,
In temper he reverted to claiming, he'd burrred the burrd, before digging the duggg
Prompting a tittering response; 'as if these creatures could ever be words.'
Yes as sure said the local as your baaaath with three 'aaahs'
In your manner of speaking, I hear lambs bleating like baa baaa baaath.

With both offended, the search was extended,
By each, to cover the faults of the other.
Finding examples which trampled good usage.
As an assault on the mother tongue
They blamed each other for damage to the language done.
The one for his stabbing consonants and guttural vowels
The other for his milk pudding of weak and listless sounds.

Word endings kept them further apart
One dropped them by habit,
The other studded them with iiss, ggss and rrrs
One lost the aiches and lengthened the vowels,
The other repeated the consonants and hardened the sounds.

But each couldn't get the other to consider,
That something not their own might be better.
So they sought applied status to determine their right
The visitor claimed the current royal speak for his side
The local, in the history of the old judges and Kings,
Not only spoke as he did but did so in verse.

But to the letter neither of them allowed the other to be better.

But hold on, if words are merely sounds,
Uttered to deliver a meaning by consonants and vowals
Then one can't be better than another, if they make sense.
To the listener skilled to hear and 'tak tent'
Communication, is all that's meant...

In truth, though he didn't want to give way,
Local understood every word visitor had to say.
Because visitor spoke in the common accent
Common to anybody with a TV or radio
Because that was the sound of broadcast media,
Where what was heard was the same as everybody else.
In that way being taught, whether it was wanted or not.

Which made the local voice distinctive
In its dialect accent and intonation.
A club to which you had to be born.
Often challenged, often scorned
But something precious that can't be learned
One among other linguistic jewels in this island crown
Sparking for its individuality,
Forever undimmed, unbowed.

THE SPOKEN WORD

Where does the spoken word go,
After it's been said?
Is it lost forever,
Once it's been heard?

Not the words of love and compliment.
They remain
Welcomed as a blessing,
Indulged and deserving,
Taken as truth when heard,
Recalled at will as first said.

Others stay to troubling effect,
The offensive remark, the lack of respect.
The slight taken without reply.
The barb picked over and analysed.
Having the last line means little,
If the response remains unsaid, undelivered.

What's worse not to have heard,
The insult not given, or the compliment not said?

COUPLES WHO FIGHT

You could tell when things were going well,
By the apologies in their conversation.
If they were talking 'sorrys' and 'my fault dears'
They were close to kisses, and making up for arrears.

Having fought to win, they were eager to lose,
Giving up gracefully, every point scored.
Till what was left between them, argument couldn't divide,
So they fell into bed, both on the same side.

But it was the revelations of personal failings,
Shared, especially when drink was taken,
This need to hear a weakness confessed,
Should be when they liked each other best.

Love for them was a form of control,
Assumed when the other was losing.
Taking need as a bounty, to give or withhold,
In forfeit of their own choosing

But in times of peace, one of them would say,
'If only it could always be like this,'
And the other would sigh and agree.
Both reflecting on the possibility,
Of being what they could never be.

Compliant, consensual, appeasing,
Moderate, temperate and calm.
Never! Not when there was a bone to be picked over
And with the addition of insult and swearing,
They were on course for their next war.

Like a street cleared when a villain appeared,
Words of kindness shrank back to being unsaid,
Behind the cruder muscled trampling fellows, who,
Found shouting the best way to be heard.

In argument like flails, they opened up the old wounds,
Accusation tipped with toxic barb,
The longer to fester, under the skin,
As the secrets they held on each other.

Spent of this language, battered by its effect,
They retreated in silence, lost for what next,
Both wanting to say what could never be said,
Until time released a... 'sorry'... faintly heard.

But welcomed as a discovery,
All forgotten what had gone before.
Their together secret, in their speedy recovery,
Clearing them to fight and forgive once more.

What they had could never be thrown away,
Always returned, as love in the lost and found.
Retrieved by one or the other... depended on,
Who was ahead in which round.

MULTIPLE CHOICE

A father was in a fashion store with his teenage daughter.
She, was choosing a dress for an occasion,
He, only there to pay, and expected to have no say,
In her choice beyond being encouraging,

Prepared for it to be a lengthy affair
He took along a book for occupation,
Knowing the main event was elsewhere.
He settled into his reading

But soon found himself distracted by the scene
Dressing room curtain thrown open and closed,
As each dress presented was tried and removed
To shrieks and sighs of disapproval.

Sharing her frustration and wanting to be encouraging
By not interfering. he buried his face deeper in the book
And suddenly found, what he believed was the root,
Cause of the problem she was facing,

She was undecided couldn't make up her mind,
Because it wasn't only her that was choosing a dress.
It was at least six of her friends,
Who weren't there at the time.

But in her head as she looked in the mirror,
Immediate for what they had to say,
About what was in, and definitely out.
And what you could or couldn't possibly like.

Their loving and loathing, was in her choosing
And one laughing at the clothes of another…
With opinions on tags, bows, buttons and drags
She hadn't yet found a dress, that didn't have one or the other.

Hers was the impossible choice. and so was the book he was reading,
Winner of the top literary prize, he had taken by recommendation,
A faltering work, unclear in narrative, repetitive and boring.
Why he asked himself had this been chosen?

This inability to come to a decision, was not a teenage freak out,
But a continuing aspect of the human proclivity.
Proving the personal choice is not independently arrived at,
But settled as a group activity.

The book reading panellist knew on the choosing,
As did his daughter with the dress,
Their first choice, their best choice,
Most accurately described themselves,
But left them unprotected,
Against the sniping of the group collective,
Hidden behind a vogue for the obscure,
Which being ill defined, leaves one inclined,
To believe in something others must know.

So his daughter goes home with a dress she'll only wear once,
And he with a book he won't finish.
Disappointed yes, but responsible, not quite
They take a small comfort from knowing,
What they had chosen was not really their choice.

KINDNESS ITSELF

Before leaving for the airport on holiday,
This man made a change in his life,
It was a self-improving decision, for him,
But he didn't tell his wife

He wanted it, to be hers to discover,
And see her delightfully surprised,
That the irritable man she had married,
Was actually a gentleman in disguise.

Kindly in manner, friendly in approach,
Courteous in demeanour, bit of a pet.
He would be that pleasant individual,
Everyone was pleased to have met.

He knew it would be a challenge in the airport departure lounge,
There were plenty there he didn't like.
From the drinking young, and the ill-disciplined child,
To the women of inordinate size, wearing tights.

It's easy to smile at people who are nice,
Why he sought out the worst to test him,
From the flip flop wearers to the baldy loud hailers,
To prove he could smile at the sight of them.

And there was another one, as they waited on check in.
A young man in a wheelchair, flaunting his disability,
Speeding past them, straight to the front of the queue,
Pleading special arrangement, and entitled facility.

That got them sniping, those around him,
Disparaging what they couldn't prove.
He would have joined in, shouting 'heh you!',
But held back on the smart remark,
To think,' What would the kindly man do?'

He wouldn't make jokes on other's misfortune,
Consider the welfare of others, He'd know what to do.
So like that man he'd become, he spoke in that tongue.
'Would you be in a wheelchair to jump a queue?'

They knew he was right by turning away,
Their jokes unworthy, they had no more to say.
He was inflated but isolated, with a hissing at his side,
His wife complaining, she had been on the point, with the woman in front,
Of swapping IDs

On the plane, a first for him, he gave the window seat to his spouse,
And there above him, and almost on top of him,
Was the apparition of all he despised.
Three irritations in one, a young woman,
With green hair and neck tattoo, effecting to try,
And shove her bag into the locker half its size

But his reaction of kindness was now instinctive,
Pausing only to say 'I think I know how,'
He was out of his seat but only as far,
As his wife's grip on his shirt would allow.

'No you're not!' she said pulling him back to hear more,
'You've been like this since we came away. What's wrong with you?'
Which he took as invitation to explain,
Decisions made, attitudes changed.
Her only response, 'Why don't you start with me?'

The hotel proved disappointing; the room shabby and small,
Its many failings pointed out by his wife,
In case he hadn't noticed them all.
In the name of peace he would have lived with it,
But that wasn't her way; she had him directed to reception,
For a must change and try for an upgrade.

His intention was to complain without losing the smile,
He had fixed on approaching reception.
But the man behind the desk, refused to look up,
Even with our man coughing quietly for attention.

And there he lost, the man he'd become.
The old one was back, temper returned.
Banging the desk with his fist, and shouting,
The receptionist woke up, to shrink back in fear,
Compelled by a stabbing finger,
To find a better apartment key.

His wife was delighted in their new sea balcony suite,
And reception proved particularly attentive,
As did the staff, who, seeing the angry guest,
Seemed almost to stand to attention

But having respect, didn't get him liked,
And kindness to others, didn't please his wife.
But when he made that decision to change,
What he never understood,
How difficult it is to be good.

THE DOG LEAD

In choosing a dog, they were mindful of,
What their choice would say about them,
And the life they led, as a couple in a suburban semi,
Well-meaning to liberal leaning, both working,
And friendly with neighbours at the weekend.

On a canine they were agreed, if not yet on the breed,
Except they both knew what they didn't want it to be,
Anything too small, broad, or terribly tall,
But they weren't opposed to a mixture of all three.

They had dismissed the thought of a classless mongrel,
A pick up from the pound, grateful and loyal to the core.
A parent less scamp with habits picked up from the street.
Like, chewing their furniture, and scratching their doors.

In truth they were inclined to the exotic,
A creature with provenance beyond these shores,
Detailed in the dog book as continental classic,
Like a foreign language spoken for the neighbours to hear.

Before they bought, in Mythology a name was sought,
One to resound literally over heath and moor.
For their charge to obey, and others to admire and declare,
'Interesting name for a dog, but then it's not from around here'

Having invoked the assistance of history,
Unlimited name search still couldn't find.
So they waited till they actually had the dog,
And by unconditioned response, let it decide.

It came up with Flossie, not in so many words,
But by its long silky ears and floppy coat,
Warm, pliant and affectionate to their touch,
Taken in by the sentiment suggesting that name they chose.

As a purchase it was expensive, for a pedigree that wasn't extensive,
In forty years it's ancestors hadn't gone fifty miles,
But bred of local farming stock, the breeder was proud to assure,
'Be none of yer fancy foreign flim flam mixtures here.'

And there by ownership they were converted,
To a preference determined by what was theirs,
Eschewing the once prized fashionable distant,
For the joined up links of local dog history.

Of which on the dog walk they were pleased to engage in small talk,
With strangers kneeling before them to ask, if the,
Creature nuzzling their crotch and licking their face,
Was pure bred? ' As the very land on which we stand' they declared.

Seeking greater opportunity, for breed superiority
They took on the competition in a local dog show
And found in the company of owners like themselves,
A people they had previously sought to ignore.

Leather and chains could hardly restrain,
Those beasts with claws and lathering jowls,
Circling and sniffing around the new bitch, while their master enquired,
If their beautiful young Flossie had yet been sired.

Hurt and diminished they fled that forum, frightened
Of where their dog was intent on leading them.
Seeking recovery, they succeeded by making a discovery ,
In a tome, a tiny footnote entry which described,
Their pure breed, as not pure but ‘corrupted,
And moreover... probably of Egyptian heritage.’

Now strangers stooping to ask, where, and what’s its name?
Are given the origin as nothing particularly specific.
Directed further to the dog’s colourful collar, are informed,
‘That spells Flossie in the hieroglyphic.’

THE SOUND BARRIER

Milly and Dean, supporting the same football team,
Did so from opposite ends of the stand.

But in sharing the game, their actions were the same,
Seated, standing, shouting, screaming for a win.

It was the away game by coach to Aberdeen,
That brought them closer than they'd ever been.
Obliged by numbers to sit together,
They found opinions identical to one another.

On the players, manager, hopes for the game,
Even before they knew each other's names.
Which shared on returning with same seats as coming,
Celebrating a win, with a wish to see each other again.

But a chasm wider than a football field
Lay between them as the great divide.
Trouncing mutual loyalty to their beloved team
They would split by a love greater than the game.

Dean was a rocker, a foot stomping ear bursting blocker,
A man of peace, turned volunteer in the music wars,
Strangling old notes, and flattenening chords,
He weaponised sound by invoking the Gods, the Spirits,
Denouncing any track without a fuck or stab in the lyrics.

Milly was mild by comparison
Her streaming leaning to ballads and light classical.
Favourite singers she held close by the tone of their voice
Warmed by their message, pinned to her heart.

Dean keen on Milly, saw her as innocence for converting,
From that dark history she had, of melody and symphony.
Which he wanted to drown in a loud and angrier sound,
Of a heavy metal goods train crossing the points.

He got off on ridiculing what wasn't his taste,
Sneering at anyone who could like 'that stuff'
Boasting of his the one true serious sound
Missing what was closest but different from him.

Milly wanting to please, dressed down for the gig as advised,
Not quite as Dean, tooled up in chains zips and leather.
But when the sound broke her ears, and the strobe took her sight,
She saw only in bits, the fits, of the man at her side,
Fist raising, head vibrating, which she tried by contrivance to follow,
By her feet making the moves, that her heart and brain refused,
Causing her to collapse at the lights.

Though Milly's tastes in music were light
Her love of hearing and sharing them ran as deep,
As his in despising the songs she liked,
It was her, not the music that suffered the hurt.

Dean leading with bands, wanted a follower,
He looked behind, she wasn't coming after.
He had given her cause to make her distance,
Not from his raging noise but his personal criticism.

Milly and Dean sit at opposite ends of the stand,
Waiting for the game to begin,
Within the blare of the club's broadcast sound
A ballad plays which he could almost admit that he likes.

Dean wants to contact Milly by text, a conciliatory act,
To record and share their first musical agreement
But as the players come on the field, the game's about to start,
The song is fading... the opportunity's lost.

AIDE MEMOIR

She had turned her past, into one of regret.
By finding evidence, supporting the acts,
Of bad behaviour and cruelties he'd used against her,
As listed in every diary she kept.

As her own witness it was the truth
A primary source, verbatim, words used,
In fleeting anger, which, pulled from the fire,
Cooled to her account in deep indelible blue.

The diary was mostly about him, the man she loved,
For better or worse; his minuted past,
Now the sadness she felt by the challenge he'd become,
Sent her back to arm herself with the facts.

How she'd been the support in everything he'd tried,
Forgiven his faults, his failed endeavours.
To hear him now spout independence of thought,
And postulate possibly managing without her...

No doubt she had inflamed herself with the reading,
Excited by the bits she'd triple underlined.
Making her yet more determined,
To get the apologies she hadn't noted at the time.

She wanted him, the man in her life,
To hear again what he was pleased to forget.
The detail contained within her writing,
Placing him forever in her debt.

He, relying on memory, could have no argument against,
What in print was true at the time.
And on claiming bias in the reporting
She responded by quoting the facts of his crimes.

But he refused to go back in time with her,
Preferring the future, however events might turn,
Making her unsure if the past man she'd sometime hated,
Wasn't better than the man he'd become.

An ageing dandy, concerned about his looks,
Yes, pleasant enough in a general way, but,
'Slippery' she had written when noticing the difference,
From the one she made in her diary days.

But in his forgetting the past by intention,
He had placed himself on a higher ground.
Looking down on his wife, diminished by her digging,
The lesser unearthed, whatever she found.

She couldn't revive the passion, the blood between the lines,
Spilled at the time of writing, now lost in words, ...consigned to,
Distant battles, former breaches of trust,
Layered to obscurity... history as dust.

That brought her to tears, mostly for the 37 years,
Of life she'd noted every single day,
All to be dismissed as self-indulgent scribbling?
No, diaries stacking a metre high, is a major literary achievement.

His words not hers, and that dried her tears,
For work he would never read, it was praise indeed.
Placed her as a historian, flawed but authentic,
Gaining him that day, a very good entry.

TALKING TO A STRANGER

There's a stranger in everybody's life, perhaps on a train,
That one you'll meet in passing, and choose to remain,
And lose an inconsequential hour or so,
In chat, and not care what you've given away.

Be a person, this stranger, someone like yourself,
Age and experience as your own.
Tuned to your pitch of conviviality,
Agreeable company to loosen your response.

By being heard without interruption or dissent,
Encouraged by that slightest approving nod,
Carrying you over beyond your own boundaries,
Of what you'd believed could never be said.

Now out for the first time, your intimacy as words spoken,
Wantonly to a stranger, who by an easy poise of caring,
Gives your shame bound hidden reserve,
Form and credibility in the sharing.

Drawn to this reception,
By a voice an agreeable echo of your own,
You lock in with the stranger,
As two adventurers in similar campaigns.

Taking you further, deeper, louder, to betray,
The one whose earlier countenance you exulted in the leaving.
The one who owns your trust, in returning,
Lesser now in this transient company.

But that's the merit of the stranger
Asking nothing of those you've left behind,
Takes all your postulations, as determined,
All your hypothesis as designed.

Lifted by the stranger's approving,
You seek a hold on something defined
Fearful that the other on leaving,
Takes your speaking their presence allowed.

But you don't agree to meet again
To do so would make a stranger a friend
Becoming known for all you said you were,
A difficult construct to defend.

Better reflect on which you'll never have to explain,
Of your conversation with a stranger, and what was gained.
Left with the deepest impression,
Wasn't to be believed in everything you said,
But simply to be listened to, and heard.

WOMAN'S OWN

Sometimes she thought she might say a little prayer,
If answered, would settle once and for all.
Her status accepted as the one she chose,
An independent woman with her own home.

She could read about herself in magazines,
Not in name but in reverence for her way
Of living, that mirrored what was 'in', and 'now'.
And that kept her afloat in the 'uncertain hour'.

Her colleagues envied her freedom as a joke,
Mothers with partners mostly, they spoke on,
Men, children, washing, cooking,
All of that, to be without, difficult for them to believe,
She wasn't still looking.

Which might be true or not, she wasn't set on being alone
Been out with others, all of her own choosing.
To go further deeper that was something else,
'What,' she asked herself, 'would she be losing?'

Sometimes she dreamt, she did nothing to prevent,
Being loved madly, taken against her better sense.
Throwing everything away, she didn't care.
Sad to wake up and not be loved,
But pleasing to know her stash was still there.

On reader's letters, of some women she was contemptuous,
Who didn't have the answer to their own questions.
The bother of one having another in her life,
Sharing her bathroom, her wardrobe, her shelves.
Against the value of cuddles, caring, affection
As if they could speak for themselves.

She believed, if asked, she had freedom of choice,
But she hadn't, not quite, when you consider,
The love and thrill of having,
Weighs heavily against the giving.
Like money in the bank has value on what it can buy,
The greater power is to leave unspent, and watch it thrive…

She had built a wall around herself,
An incomplete protection that still allowed
The possibility of someone breaking in,
And stealing what she had for herself.
Which to prevent,
She raised higher, the standard required,
To have as much, and more,
Than everything as a girl she had dreamt of,
And something extra to be doubly sure.

The route to happiness was in every article,
Which she read purely as entertainment.
But the section which on reflection,
She considered the most interesting,
Was that on the puzzle page.
Where by way of a conundrum her own question was put,
The one she never liked to ask... ‘When,
If one is indivisible, is it doubled when shared?’
Answers please on the last page.

CLUB MEMBERSHIP

I never thought of myself as being judged,
Until I joined the local bowling club.
And there, among the membership
Found myself, as described by others.

I got the hint of it, when a fellow bowler being kind,
Assured me, unlike some, he considered me a friend.
Which as an assurance given and taken in the same breath,
Left me unsure what it was to be liked.

Considering the effort I made to be included,
By laughing over drinks at the bar.
And taking the insults, resulting,
Being called an old goat and worse, which is,
A term of endearment at this club.

After a month of this I came to know,
Friendship was mine to make, not theirs to bestow.
I had to decide who I wanted to sit beside
And by division, increase the coefficient,
By limiting my choice.

You see, the Club as a whole, is made up of sides,
Cliques as sometimes called; not evident on the green,
Where teams are democratically chosen,
But loudly exclusive in the bar and lounge
Where seating is by preferred association.

But this was the currency in which they traded,
A proclaimed disdain for those not themselves.
And that kept them close, provided the jokes
As the distance from others like myself.

From my seat alone I looked for a friend
And found one in the mutual dislike of another.
That sour ingredient that sweetened, our conversation,
And brought us closer together.

In the monogrammed blazer,
One member looks much like another.
One club on the day of the prizes.
But on closer inspection you'll find
They all come in different sizes.

And it's still new members welcome,
Make friends, join the club.
But if you're thinking to be in our side of it,
Sorry but, we're already full up.

FRIENDSHIP?

Friends for life, they said,
You never see one without the other.
Until one loose word, overheard
Cast it all asunder, after 23 years.

That word, spoken by one, misheard by the other,
From a third party who didn't know either,
Came as a whisper, translating as thunder,
Broke as a storm, cracking,
A cleft in the middle,
Of a friendship, biscuit thin.

But that weakness was there from the start,
They met up as habit and convenience.
Thieves of each other's time,
Never held a promise to each other
Never anything, that couldn't be talked apart.

And that's friendship,
You think it'll stand whatever.
No irons in the fire
No money in the ring,
No sex to hold it together.

Countless examples of it,
Friends and relations, ending in tears.
Crossing the street, refusing to meet,
On a slight, which on the night,
Might have been ignored.
Still burning, after forty years.

But they liked each other right enough,
From schooldays to the pub.
Went holidays together with their wives,
Knew the names of each other's kids.

Their old pals scene, wasn't an act,
Locked together, fierce in their criticism of others,
They were solid to dismiss what wasn't themselves,
To be nurses to their own shortcomings.

But the secrets they kept from each other,
Were what mattered in their lives.
How much money they had in the bank,
How often they slept with their wives.

Most of the thoughts one had on the other,
Couldn't be safely expressed.
Not the envy of how much the other had more,
Not the scorn for the manners, the one had less.
A hive of irritations, discreetly repressed.

That outlet was managed by going home to their wives.
And listing what annoyed them, each about the other.
The wives who had heard it before, said nothing but knew,
What sounded like hate, would meet again as before.

Until offence was taken,
On something which was nothing at all.
But from nothing came silence,
And from silence came space,
Which widened between them,
Until from a distance, there was no trace,

Of a 23-year-old friendship,
Which could have been saved,
If more words had been used,
Not with politeness and pleasance of manner,
But in argument, surviving it, and sharing the truce.

A STUDENT MATURES

Lily at forty, coming late to learning,
With a husband and teenage son,
Experienced less fear of her academic undertaking,
Than the domestic she would be leaving undone.

In her life to date as a working mother on flexible time,
She managed the house, looked after the men,
By an after work round of cooking and cleaning,
With the full shop reserved for the weekend.

Now that her occupation would be in reading and writing,
Classes attending, lectures delivered.
Time taken up with what didn't appear to be work, she feared,
If the real was being sacrificed for the perceived.

But she needn't have worried, by her husband's enthusiasm,
That her intelligence be placed to greater effect,
In status improved with honours degree,
Increased earnings and greater respect.

How all this was to be achieved, by the men it was agreed,
Housework under their command, providing coffee on demand,
Would be a service, leaving her free , to study when she pleased,
After the shopping and making the evening meal.

It gave her a degree of assurance from those she loved most,
Willing her to succeed and be the best.
What she hadn't quite evaluated in the transition,

How much of herself, would be lost in the process.
For the good and the willing that was in her,
Would not easily be subdued.
The anchor of responsibility she bore,
Not easily weighed.

She would have to make the effort to identify as a student,
And not as wife, mother, keeper of the keys.
But she worried the effect this would have on the men,
Their needs much with her, she still wanted them to be pleased.

Her first test came in the peaceful setting,
Of a warm summer's day in the garden.
Coffee provided, her reading beside her,
Conditions perfect for her subject's absorption.

And even better that her practical mind,
Was cleared of everything needing to be done.
On a programme of advanced setting, her study more effective,
Knowing, she had a washing in the machine.

She read with fluidity, noting in the margins,
Words as constructs, material for an essay begun.
But what later appeared, with her thoughts interfered,
The image of that washing lying damp in the drum.
(In her house previously, this had never been done)

She could have steeled herself, resisted a triviality,
Pledged her mind deeper to her study analysis.
But a gentle breeze lifting the page, slight but insisting,
Reminding her of the great drying day she was missing.

Yes, Lilly had to confess, her best study aid, was the work done first.
She had tried believing her men when they claimed,
This was tidied and that was cleaned.
Not wanting to lose their support, she didn't make a fight,
But picked up after them late at night,
Doubling her workload for peace of mind.

In her study at the top of the house,
She wrote out of sight but not of sound.
The voice of her husband berating her son,
For his share of the dishes that hadn't been done.
Rose to her anguish, making her scream for silence,
And lose track of what she was working on.

Taking refuge in the uni library, she found herself among other,
Students with a need to share and make friends.
Learned subject development continues after hours at the bar,
Drawn by convention, she merged her life with theirs.

As a mature student she had much to give,
From experience of living, and much to learn,
On equal rights of the individual
For whom she marched en group to become,
First to learn, leaving early to make her men's dinner,
That, in the university house, was never done.

Then at home it was independence all round.
Her teenage son left for the first time.
Freed by her absence, her husband took his own line,
Sourcing ingredients, and making meals, when he wasn't eating out.

As a student she was happy to come home when she chose,
And talk of those, her husband had never seen.
As a wife, when he was late, she still worried,
But could no longer ask him where he'd been.

It was the freedom's chill that swirled around them,
Cooled the sweat on her forced labour.
Lost her control of the kitchen, she once ruled,
To occasionally, come home to a cooked meal.

The domestic was solved by the inclusion of another,
A working mother like herself, but younger in need of money.
A stranger with a key; bathroom, bedroom, didn't amount to care,
But a house is more easily cleaned when the living is elsewhere.

MEET THE WEATHER

A visitor coming to Scotland for the first time,
Looking to find, what had been left behind,
By his people, since they were last here and cleared.

He had given himself a week to take in five hundred years.
Ambitious but not overly so, in a small country with good roads.
He planned for one museum a day, two castles, and three Bens in the week,
That, with the locals speak, for authenticity,
Should wrap up his claim to genuine ancestry.

He stepped off the plane to some rain,
For which he was well prepared,
But not for the Atlantic depression,
Which had followed him over,
In the name of low pressure,
To open up above where he stayed.

There followed days of downpours,
Burst riverbanks and flooding.
An attempted hill walk, aborted,
When the rain
Met the hail coming upwards.

With ferry boats cancelled, and travel suspended,
The museum proved its worth as a shelter,
From where he could dry out, to read about,
The places he planned to see, but couldn't,
For the mist cut the mountains, and shortened the view,
To a box of grey, from which, by the end of the week,
He was glad to be set free.

Only on the day of his leaving, the sun made a lasting appearance,
And did so in spectacular style,
A cloudless blue from horizon to the heavens, and in for the week,
Marked only by the speck of a silver streak,
Taking our visitor back home.
Where from above he had his first views of Scotland,
Mainland and islands, in shades of blue, purple and green.
A pattern of the mountains he had never climbed, lochs and glens he had never seen.

But the image stayed with him, and took him back the following year,
Plus a week for he now knew summer's beginning.
Only to be told on arrival, the scorcher he'd missed,
As he scurried out of the blustery showers.
Which he took personally as if he was targeted,
By spending more time in hotel bar,
Asking the locals, not about the kilt the plaid and the dirk,
But about the weather, and how to get rid of it.

The locals were phlegmatic on the subject,
One said, best come in May the other in June, and a third declared,
You always get a good week in September.
The only time on which they all agreed, 'don't come at the Glasgow Fair.'

Back for a third year to complete,
The research he had aimed for in the week.
With waterproof cape, knee high boots, and sou wester,
None of which, he had any need.

As he lay deep sprung on a bed of hillside heather,
By wild flowers, his hat shielding the sun,
So still, in sleep he was taken back,
To find the key to where it had all begun
If this land was his land, so was the weather,
As one had been formed, each by the other
That brought him closer than he had ever been,
More than artefacts, more than the little screen.
To be in the same rain from which his people took shelter,
Know the storm winds that bent them under,
See the white clouds give way to a glorious sun,

Why he would be back again,
To welcome the weather as much as the land.
For that was his contact, the link in his people's chain,
As one in passing, making what remains.

THE COMPOSITION OF THE ORCHESTRA

An orchestra is composed mostly of those,
Who, as children, stayed in, while we played out.
They were seriously taught,
Finger placing and breath control,
While we kicked a ball against a wall.
They took up parent's endeavour,
We wore ours down until allowed,
To hand back clarinets and violins,
For the next unwilling.

But we developed quicker, the untutored,
Knew the streets, sport, swearing,
Long in advance, of the music case carriers,
Who walked quickly, head bowed,
Embarrassed by their burden.
A childhood sacrificed to a secret code.
Separated from the mob by their tuition,
They grew older and more serious.

But now as an occasional concert goer,
I applaud them for their skills.
Lately having learned to appreciate music,
It's they who have the means to capture me.
Their young years kept indoors, paid off,
I pay to hear them.
But on a summer's evening, after a days work,
I never stay awake beyond the second movement.
Succumbing to an easier pleasure,
I lack the greater discipline still.

LOVE'S THE UNKNOWING

If I could look at others,
And see what I want to see,
Would that determine,
What I am, and what I want to be?
Their truth uncovered, giving a clear view,
I'd have the exact on everybody,
Friends I would come to know,
For what they were hiding not what they wanted to show.
I'd have their secrets,
Mine to control,
The better to know,
What they can't withold.
Making for,
An honest, understanding,
A trust based on facts.
Real friends at last,
Without the acts.
Mine to call out the poseur and the fraud.
Mine to determine,
What can't be gainsaid.
But...
There's the responsibility
Seen for what I saw,
I'd be judged on my judging,
My interpretation of my law.

Their shame revealed, at my bidding?
Would that be me?
No!
I'd be kind and forgiving,
Knowing them as myself, and myself as they are,
I'd understand what I shouldn't see,
And rise on the good that says about me.
Or...
Would it be too horrible, not being able to blink
Against the detail of it,
The scale of it,
The bright hard nail of it,
Sharp as the sun
Forced to look on with their buttons undone?
No.
I'd rather be ignorant, how I was born,
Blind and trusting,
Not knowing if they were genuine or having me on.
Love's the unknowing, so let them be,
Wrapped tight, and unknowable,
Especially those closest to me.

BAD HABITS

If that ‘bad habit’ was a thug or a villain,
Of course you’d want to get rid of him,
And know exactly the way, right!
You’d call him out, tag him, take him,
Break him, beat him out of your sight.

You’d boast to friends on what you left for dead,
That bastard habit had your life in debt.
Now you’re clear, shot of that dependence,
Was he the shit you once befriended?

You’re strong on what you’ve beaten
Positive; you’re back in control.
Everybody knows you stood up to the crap
Taken what was yours, you never look back.

But if that ‘bad habit’ was a good friend,
What you going to do there then?
The pal you wouldn’t live without,
You now want that friendship to end?

You’d have to ask yourself why, because,
No harm to you was ever intended.
Nothing demanding of your attention,
He was a buddy, only by your invitation.

But you had reliance as a bond
The effect of sharing brought its rewards.
A sometime controlled way of being, but,
You revelled in being occasionally taken.

So now you're clear of that so called 'bad habit',
But you're still with remembered times.
You know it's better to have lost the villain, than the friend,
Only one of them you'd even consider taking back,
If it was your decision, which one you liked best.

IN CONVERSATION

They met respectful of each other's speaking,
If one spoke, the other listened.
Like two mannered diplomats,
Cautious and contained
Fearful of upsetting
A balance not yet obtained,
But in seeking to be pleasing,
And receiving the same,
Kind words meeting with kinder,
They found in voice, a desire to remain.
In conversation,
They made their own
A weave of words spinning
A protected zone.
Allowed them softly
To better explore,
Who they were, and what they hoped to be.
Revealing within the closer exchange,
The slip of intimacy gained.
From conversation,
Eager to lock in, what had become,
Words crossed at shuttle speed, mostly unheard.
Talking had become, a babble unrestrained
Language laced with laughter, translating as joy.
All the better the means to employ,

Their need to hold fast,
Beyond conversation.
More what was meant,
And less what was said.
And so it ended,
Sudden as that,
Silence descending as dark.
Lips closed, stopped them speaking.
What more to be said,
A kiss has the greater meaning.

THOUGHTS UNSAID

Looks like anger, sounds like contempt,
Spiced with humour, nothing seriously meant.
Tradesmen's talk.
I sat in on their arguments,
Heard them debate,
An apprentice with adults,
At their tea break take on the world.

To which I would contribute,
If allowed to deliver,
My timed interjection, opinion prepared.
Between their crossfire of words,
I had something to say,
Enough to disrupt the chatter,
And hopefully be praised.

If asked,
Which I never was.
Looking for the prompt which didn't arrive,
Swallowing my own voice,
As the topic moved on.
This youth among men,
Didn't battle to be heard, but instead,
Took in silence, the hurt of ignoring,
Retreating unsaid.

Accorded authority by experience,
Some tradesmen seek,
To press on a fluid mind,
Their own, and what they hold dear.
A mixture of what is, and what shouldn't be.
Unsupported in company of their peers,
But given in solid form to the young, constrained to believe.
I, silenced by this order,
Held them in contempt.
Their ridicule and dismissal,
Losing the argument,
I knew better, could make more sense,
Mocking their weakness,
In dumb insolence.

Now as an adult without restraint,
I make sure I'm heard in argument.
Robust, concise, assured,
Not one to be ignored.
But losing patience with some who don't agree
I dismiss their contention as lesser than me,
Using words such as 'ridiculous' and 'nonsense'.
I get the audience required,
For my own and what I hold dear.

Which reminds me of those who silenced me,
The old dogmatists who could never hear,
A word in opposition to their own.
Is this now me?
Easily dismissing what comes softly
and shrinks from the fight.
To be on top, to be in the right?

What have I missed?
What might I have learned from thoughts unsaid,
What has been lost by this need to be heard?
That I'll never know.

LAYABOUT

To drift without measure,
And lay a crazy path.
To have no direction
Or calculating math.
To be the result of losing your way,
Closing bewildered,
The reckoning of every day.
To find sleep the rescue from cliff edge
And dreams, the means,
Of renewal
Shedding everything learned,
As dust from the track
Experience, thrown off,
As the clothes on your back,
To break free
And fall like a feather,
Caught by a breeze
To land wherever.
You are the child of instinct,
Naked and unknowing.
Courage enough to cover the planet.

A PEBBLE ON A STONY BEACH

On her last day of a company break, away,
She walked on the sand as it touched the sea,
Looking for a pocket-sized pebble, a keepsake
When she no longer was but might wish to be-

Reminded of a moment in the space of a week,
That spread in thought as the blush on her cheek,
Of a kindness given, a compliment received
As rare as the pebble she picked among the stones.

A younger man walking a dog on this solitary beach,
In passing gave her a smile, and praised her looks,
As fresh and clear against the breeze blown from the sea,
And 'just the tonic' he needed for that day.

She by instinct turned away as she had been taught,
To regard flattery as motive for something else.
Best met with a hardened stare which she prepared,
But the stranger passed, expecting nothing from his remarks.

The distance they made from each other
Allowed her a pause to re-consider, the line,
About her clear complexion and youth,
And retrieve from that nonsense, something of the truth.

Which made her want to look in a mirror,
To be again at the sea, smile to provoke the compliment,
Mime the words, which at home would never be heard,
Nor encouraged to be believed.

Separated from her partner on the business trip,
Seeing more from a distance than close up.
Absence brought her the opportunity,
For that moment to last longer than the week.

Why the pebble, which, as she showed him, he said stone,
Taking and turning it over as weight in his hands,
Questioning what was the point of it, quickly,
Losing interest and tossing it back to her.

She wasn't hurt, by what she expected
Having hoped he would ask why,
As her prompt to reveal and immediately deny,
The importance of what, she said, meant nothing to her

It was how she parried his cynicism
By detailing exactly the comments on the beach,
Then laughingly dismissing the sense of it,
As a vanity aroused, she could never take seriously.

It took the sting our of any scornful retort
By getting there first, about her looks, with a joke.
But the compliment retracted as soon as said
Remained as something added, value accrued

Her objective in dismissing what was freely given,
To provoke his protest, that none of it was strictly untrue,
That the stranger's sentiments might be his own,
Spoken, but too close to be heard.

Why the pebble as worthless, served a purpose
To reinstate what habit had dulled.
To raise the bar on which they both might aspire.
To compliment and lose nothing by it.

LOOKING FOR LOVE

He, desperate to be in love again,
Prepared himself to fall, without hesitation,
Into any situation, on the slightest provocation
And be willingly shaped to another's inclination.

It was a sacrifice he was prepared to make
To lose himself to a woman's bidding,
Based on previous affairs, previous mistakes,
Give up taking, to take up the giving-

-to another, that which he had stolen before,
By indifference, self-regard and lack of respect
Now that part of him was excised by regret,
He was the more gentle and considerate prospect.

The means by which he aimed to attract
A woman of his own age or younger
As himself, self-reliant, confident and single
Someone who doesn't frighten children.

How it began tentative and non-demanding,
She carried her shopping, he opened the door.
The coffee they shared the means to explore
Where they were and what had gone before.

But it didn't take long before this fallen man,
Was gripped by the passion he knew from the past.
Revived in him now, as the older yet stronger,
That longing he could have for someone else.

All this from opposite ends of a small table.
In juvenile behaviour he made her laugh,
And took from her laughing, happiness, shared,
Like a double act on their own clown stage.

He was caught in the throes of love's progression,
Which began when a look was enough,
Leading to a conversation in which closeness of speaking,
Formed the prologue to his visceral need to touch.

But his love's desire to get under her clothes,
Was stymied by the fact they were never alone.
Her friendly manner to all she encountered,
Meant that at best he was one of a number-

-in this circle of friends she had around her
As protection against the single man, who
By experience she learned, came with intent,
To dominate, and take what he wanted from her.

As much as she was independent of living,
She avoided having to make decisions.
Wanting to please, and not hurt by refusing requests,
She feared being taken against her own interests.

But she had her dreams; being ravished by some figure unseen,
Consumed in body heat shared, -until reality intervened,
Waking in her own bed alone but relieved, not to have,
That twelve stone man lying on top of her.

For him as one of several who circled around her,
Suspicious of the others for signs of favour,
Self-induced passion proved a lesson sadly learned,
What it was like to love and be liked in return.

THE SMALL OF A WOMAN'S BACK

I once lived in the small of a woman's back,
knew my way around surrendered hills,
breathed the deep scent of a flowers garden,
in that countries' space I grew to fill,
and follow where sensation led me
my right as freedom to roam,
picked at will fruits which appealed to me
trampling where I might have sown
until returning to that place of 'special interest'
I found the path chosen and worn by habit,
'Under Protection' and 'Closed' to me
which obliged me to view from a remembered state
admire from a distance that beautiful landscape
in recovery by being untouched, and long to return,
not by establishing a right of contact
but softly surreptitiously landing
In the small of that woman's back.

WHAT REMAINS

Not yet left school, I had already left my interest in learning,
In pursuit of my new passion, adding bulk to my slight physique.
Saving up to buy weights, I looked for another method of building muscle,
And found one on top of a railway wagon filled with coal,
To be unloaded by shovel on to a waiting lorry .

My father who drove the lorry,
Allowed me first pick from top of the nuggets peak.
I leaped to the task.
The men laughed.
I fed on their laughter as I dug into the coal,
Furious to earn their praise.

I tired quickly, and they took over.
Working deep into the void of the wagon,
They lowered themselves, by removing the coal they stood on,
up and over the high side until they were on steel.
I watched to admire their adult strength

One in particular.
The youngest, the fittest, working on while the others took a break.
He was the athlete among them, the lifter of weights.
I took him for my champion.
When my father commented on the same man's shovelling prowess,
I willed him to say more, arousing the passion in me for the man,
And the ownership I had taken of him.

The wagon emptied, the men smoked and talked among themselves.
My man, modest among them, no longer distinct from the others.
But I knew his test would come again, another hour,
another wagon, and there in that small arena he would again be the gladiator.

Later in life I left strength building and returned to learning.
With education I had the cleverer take on what had been.
I now saw my former gladiator as a capitalist dupe,
Conned into working harder by a few
choice words in praise of his strength.
He had been fooled as had I.

But what I admired had not been lost,
Champion at shovelling coal,
The image remained.
He could not be beaten,
Nor will he be.
I hold him still as hero in my time.

APPROPRIATE CONTACT

The closest I'd ever come to a woman
was when I asked a girl to dance,
and she accepted by placing her hand in mine,
making us a couple among others
waiting for the band to commence.

I don't know her name, hadn't seen her before,
I'm attracted by her looks, that's all I know...
She, without choosing, allowed me the dance,
Prepared to be polite for as long as it lasts.
But we're already beyond good manners,
the stuffy behaviour of awkward strangers.
We're united by interlocking fingers.

And we're going on from there.

Within conventions boundaries we are encouraged
to place our free hands on each other's bodies,
as a form of legitimate contact.
She, with hers on my back,
mine on her waist, resting on the hip;
in plain sight we two who hardly speak,
as close as lovers begin to dance.

Now here, conversation is expected
as two social beings interacting.
but there's the difficulty, 'chat' usually depends
on shared interests, and mutual friends,
but we have none, nothing but a corporeal presence,
moving together without explanation, and almost as one.

Because talk is junior to sensation
the brain is taken by image translating;
The contact of her skin, the perfume, the full of her dress
against my legs, my hand on the fabric at her waist,
prompting me by touch to guess,
what she is wearing underneath.

I am consumed by the closeness of a woman
but I don't want it to last;
the four minutes of the dance
will be more than enough. I know she'll agree.
When that music comes to an end
We'll excuse ourselves and never meet again.

Why?

Because the head has overtaken the heart
making judgement on what has passed
for required conversation; tradition has me pitched as the opener;
'a comment perhaps on her dress, her looks, the band, something
inconsequential even bland, funny yes, that's better but not...'
what I don't care to remember, stuck in my throat, what I wanted
to say
but managed instead... a half sentence, maybe... then... in
consequence… stuttered to silence.

But I find my voice in thanking her for the dance,
relief having giving me the confidence I didn't have,
when up close and sharing body heat with breathing.
Which now alone, I have with me as a preserve,
the contact image to sugar being lost for words,
To heighten the sense of where I have been
and torment myself with my imaginings
I might never be there again.

Lightning Source UK Ltd.
Milton Keynes UK
UKHW011039181122
412419UK00001B/11

9 781803 812281